IS-106.16: Workplace Violence Awareness Training 2016

By

Fema

1/4/2016

Course Summary

IS-106.16 - Workplace Violence Awareness Training 2016

Introduction

Preventing Workplace Violence is a growing concern within FEMA and throughout the Federal Government.

Workplace Violence is often thought of as a physical attack. But it may also include threats, intimidation, and other disruptive behavior, oral or written statements, and gestures or expressions that communicate a direct or indirect threat of physical harm.

During incident response, there are many factors that contribute to the risk of Workplace Violence. For example, FEMA employees are often in direct contact with incident victims, whose tempers may flare if expectations cannot be met. Even among FEMA employees, confrontation may arise when exhaustion levels, pressure, and emotions run high.

This course is designed to help you recognize common warning signs of violent behavior, understand the steps you can take to prevent Workplace Violence, or effectively respond if it occurs. You can make a difference and help ensure the personal safety and security of all FEMA Facilities staff and incident victims.

Course Overview

The goal of this course is to give employees awareness of violence in the workplace, how to recognize the warning signs, and what actions to take to prevent or minimize violence. The objectives of this course are:

- Define Workplace Violence in accordance with the FEMA 123-14 Directive (replaces FEMA 1200.1 Directive) and the DHS memo referenced in the course.
- List the four types of Workplace Violence.
- Identify the three warning sign levels related to potential Workplace Violence.
- List the action steps taken in response to workplace violence.
- Identify ways to prevent Workplace Violence.

DHS/FEMA Policy

This section deals with FEMA's policy on Workplace Violence, and how preventing violence is everyone's responsibility.

Policy Regarding Workplace Violence

As noted in policy guidance, DHS/FEMA prohibits acts of violence, threats, harassment, intimidation, or otherwise disruptive behavior by or against FEMA staff. Examples of other prohibited Workplace Violence include homicide, physical assaults, stalking, domestic violence, bullying, and emotional abuse.

This policy applies to all FEMA employees, contractors, and personnel from other agencies that are performing official duties in support of FEMA's mission.

All reports of incidents involving Workplace Violence will be taken seriously and dealt with appropriately. Individuals who commit such acts may be removed from the premises and may be subject to disciplinary action, criminal penalties, civil litigation, or all of the above.

Employee Responsibilities: Respect

It is the responsibility of all employees, including other persons supporting FEMA's mission, to respect all persons and government property.

- Refrain from behavior that could be perceived as threatening, harassing, intimidating, or dangerous to yourself or others.
- Cooperate and participate in efforts recommended to resolve workplace concerns.
- Attend violence in the workplace training. Training is mandatory for FEMA employees, and attendance is encouraged for other individuals employed at FEMA facilities.

Employee Responsibilities: Reporting

Report violent acts or threats of violence to your immediate supervisor, the Office of the Chief Security Officer, Internal Investigation Branch, or the Employee and Labor Relations Division. Information regarding a threat of a harmful act, where you reasonably believe that the circumstances may lead to a harmful act, should be reported immediately.

Refrain from reporting false information or making unfounded complaints against others. Any individual who knowingly makes a false report or unfounded complaint may be subject to disciplinary action and/or referral to the Office of the Inspector General for investigation and possible criminal prosecution.

Director Responsibilities

Administrators, Deputy Administrators, Regional Administrators Chief Counsel, Inspector General, and Federal Coordinating Officers (or designees):

- Will ensure that a Crisis Management Plan has been developed that meets local needs for each facility under their management control.
- Will ensure that a Crisis Management Team has been appointed and trained at each facility under their organizational control. Teams will be staffed by full-time security personnel if assigned to the facility.
- Will ensure that all employees in their organization have attended mandatory training on Workplace Violence.
- Must promote an environment that strives to minimize the likelihood of violence at work.

Management Responsibilities: Environment

Management must promote an environment that strives to minimize the likelihood of violence for employees under their supervision by:

- Demonstrating respect for all employees and holding them accountable for their behavior.
- Refusing to tolerate harmful, threatening, intimidating, harassing, disruptive, or other inappropriate behavior in the workplace.
- Encouraging employees to seek appropriate assistance through programs such as Alternative Dispute Resolution (ADR).
- Attending violence in the workplace training and ensuring that subordinate staff attends the training, as well. Managers and supervisors are encouraged to take advantage of other training opportunities to improve skills in areas such as human relations, interpersonal communications, conflict management, and defusing hostility.

Management Responsibilities: Observations

Managers and supervisors are expected to monitor, assess, and respond to employee complaints, credible reports of threats, questionable behavior, and prohibited conduct. For example, managers should:

- Be alert for the warning signs of inappropriate or prohibited behavior.
- Immediately report employee complaints and other questionable actions to the security staff and their supervisors.
- In instances of imminent danger, immediately contact 911 and Federal Protective Service as soon as possible at 1-866-547-7056 and any other appropriate law enforcement authorities and a member of the local Crisis Management Team.

Management Responsibilities: Confidentiality

Managers and supervisors must preserve the confidentiality of employee complaints. For example:

- Share information only with those who have a need to know in order to carry out official government business.
- Protect incident reports, related information, and the privacy of persons involved, just as in other sensitive and confidential personnel matters.

However, there is an exception when there is evidence of a direct threat or potential harm to self or others.

Office of the Chief Component Human Capital Officer (OCCHCO)

Employees and managers can always receive advisement and assistance from the Office of the Chief Component Human Capital Officer (OCCHCO) regarding inappropriate behavior in the workplace. Inappropriate behavior includes fighting as well as threatening, intimidating, harassing, disruptive, or other harmful behavior.

The OCSO provides assistance to supervisors and managers regarding disciplinary and/or adverse actions for inappropriate behavior at work, and coordinates with the Office of Chief Counsel concerning disciplinary and/or adverse actions for inappropriate behavior.

- You may also Contact FEMA Office of the Chief Security Officer, Internal Investigation Branch at 1-866-847-7056 to provide assistance and guidance.

Types of Workplace Violence

This section deals with the different categories of Workplace Violence.

Types of Workplace Violence

Workplace Violence falls into four broad categories:

- Type 1: Violence by criminals.
- Type 2: Violence by customers.
- Type 3: Violence by employees.
- Type 4: Violence by related parties.

Types of Workplace Violence: Violence by Criminals

Type 1 violence includes violent acts by criminals who have no other connection with the workplace, but enter to commit robbery or another crime.

Such violence accounts for the vast majority (nearly 80 percent) of workplace homicides. The motive is usually theft.

In many cases, the criminal is carrying a gun or other weapon, increasing the likelihood that the victim will be killed or seriously wounded.

This type of violence most frequently affects particular occupational groups such as taxi drivers (who have by far the highest risk of being murdered), late-night retail or gas station clerks, others who are on duty at night, those who work in isolated locations or dangerous neighborhoods, and those who carry or have access to cash.

Types of Workplace Violence: Violence by Customers

Type 2 includes violence directed at employees by customers, clients, patients, students, inmates, or any others for whom an organization provides services.

Such violence can be very unpredictable. It may be triggered by an argument, anger at the quality of service, denial of service, delays, or some other precipitating event.

Disaster Recovery Centers and Individual Assistance or Community Relations field personnel can be especially vulnerable to this type of violence.

Types of Workplace Violence: Violence by Employees

The third type of Workplace Violence consists of acts committed by a present or former employee. Such violence may be directed against coworkers, supervisors, or managers.

Although violence by employees is very rare, the pressures, long hours, and working conditions of deployments may increase stress and interfere with an individual's ability to cope.

Types of Workplace Violence: Violence by Related Parties

Type 4 includes violence committed in the workplace by someone who doesn't work there, but has a personal relationship with an employee—for example, an abusive spouse or domestic partner.

In such cases, there is a greater chance that warning signs were observed, but ignored. Coworkers or managers may have believed the signs were not important or were "none of their business."

Warning Signs

This section deals with the different warning signs of violence, and the immediate steps you may need to take as a result.

Observing Behavior and Warning Signs

Often, people's behaviors may be indicators of potential Workplace Violence. Common indicators include intimidating behavior, such as argumentative exchanges, making direct or indirect threats, and sabotaging or stealing equipment.

In some extreme situations, you may witness sharp spikes of anger, while other warning signs may be directed inwards. You should be concerned if someone becomes very depressed or withdrawn.

In this part of the course, you'll learn more about the warning signs so that you can help prevent workplace violence.

Behavior and Warning Signs

Regardless of the type of workplace violence, the chances for prevention improve with increased awareness of potential warning signs and rapid response to a potential problem.

No one can predict human behavior, and there is no specific "profile" of a potentially dangerous individual. However, studies indicate that incidents of violence are usually preceded by patterns of behavior or other activities that may serve as warning signs.

While there are no fail-safe measures to ensure that violence will never occur, early action and intervention can serve to defuse a potentially dangerous situation and minimize the risk of violence.

Warning Sign Levels

Warning signs of violent behavior may be classified into three levels.

Not everyone exhibiting warning signs will become violent. However, no warning sign should be completely ignored. Any one or combination of warning signs, at any level, may indicate a potentially violent situation.

Warning Signs: Level 1—Intimidation

In Level 1, the person exhibits intimidating behaviors that are:

- Discourteous/disrespectful,
- Uncooperative, and/or
- Verbally abusive.

Level 1 Warning Signs: Employee Responses

In Level 1 situations, the employee should:

- Observe and document the behavior in question.
- Report his or her concerns to the supervisor to seek help in assessing and responding to the situation.

One technique for addressing the situation in a respectful manner and establishing limits with the offending coworker is the use of "I" statements, such as:

- "I don't like shouting. Please lower your voice."
- "I don't like it when you point your finger at me."
- "I want to have a good working relationship with you."

Level 1 Warning Signs: Supervisor Responses

The supervisor should meet with the offending employee to discuss the concerns.

If the offending employee is the reporting employee's immediate supervisor, the employee should notify the next level of supervision.

If the offending person is not an employee, the supervisor of the employee reporting the incident is still the appropriate individual to receive the information and provide initial response.

Warning Signs: Level 2—Escalation

During Level 2, the person escalates the situation. For example, he or she may:

- Argue with customers, vendors, coworkers, or management.
- Refuse to obey agency policies or procedures.
- Sabotage equipment or steal property for revenge.
- Verbalize wishes to hurt coworkers or management.
- Stalk, harass, or show undue focus on another person.
- Make direct or indirect threats to coworkers or management (in person, in writing, by phone).
- View himself or herself as victimized by management (me against them) and talk about "getting even."

Level 2 Warning Signs: Employee Responses

When faced with Level 2 warning signs, the employee should:

- Call Federal Protective Service at 1-877-437-7411 or 9-1-1, if warranted.
- Contact FEMA Office of the Chief Security Officer, Internal Investigation Branch as soon as possible at 1-866-847-7056.
- Secure the safety of self and others, if necessary.
- Immediately contact the supervisor.
- Document the observed behavior in question.

Level 2 Warning Signs: Supervisor Responses

The supervisor should consult with officials, such as functional area experts, for help in assessing/responding to the situation.

When meeting with an offending employee, the supervisor should:

- Avoid an audience.
- Remain calm, speaking slowly, softly, and clearly.
- Ask the employee to sit, to see if he or she is able to follow directions.
- Ask questions about the complaint, such as:
    - What can you do to regain control of yourself?
    - What can I do to help you regain control?
    - What do you hope to gain by committing violence?
    - Why do you believe you need to be violent to achieve that goal?
- Direct aggressive tendencies into other behaviors, so the employee sees that there are choices about how to react.

Further Guidance from the Office of Personnel Management (OPM)

Experts say that while it's difficult to come up with a precise profile of a worker who could turn violent, there are a number of warning signs employees and employers should watch for:

1. Watch out for direct or veiled threats.
2. Look out for intimidating or aggressive behavior.
3. Be alert to employees bringing weapons to the workplace or employees who seem overly fascinated with firearms and/or violence.
4. Pay attention to employees who appear to be going through a difficult time.
5. Look for employees who suddenly start showing up late or not showing up at all that previously were always on time.
6. Pay attention to workers who show contempt for fellow workers and or superiors.
7. Look for workers who are acting abnormally or paranoid.

Employers should:

1. Encourage employees to report suspicious or threatening incidents at work.
2. Provide training in stress management for workers.
3. Offer employee assistance programs to help workers deal with stress.

Crisis Plan

According to the U.S. Office of Personnel Management all employers should have a Crisis Plan in place to deal with the worst possible situations. OPM recommends the following:

1. Escape routes: Designated escape routes for all employees
2. Codes: Code words to alert personnel of a threatening situation
3. Check- in times: Regular check-in times for employees or supervisors who work alone or in isolated areas
4. Resource guide: A resource directory containing all important telephone numbers, referral sources, consultants, and emergency procedures
5. Chain of command: A clearly defined chain of command to insure that the proper people are notified in the event of an emergency
6. Planned responses: Pre-planned response units of management and security personnel, violence drills and simulations incorporated into all safety training programs
7. Regular training: Regular in-service training sessions designed to increase employee awareness and readiness.

Visit the U.S. Office of Personnel Management web site (http://www.opm.gov) for more information on workplace violence.

Warning Signs: Level 3—Further Escalation

Level 3 usually results in some form of emergency response. In such cases, the person displays intense anger resulting in:

- Suicidal threats.
- Physical fights or assaults of coworker(s) or manager(s).
- Damage or destruction of property.
- Concealment or use of a weapon to harm others.
- Display of extreme rage or physically aggressive acts, throwing or striking objects, shaking fists, verbally cursing at others, pounding on desks, punching walls, or angrily jumping up and down.

Level 3 Warning Signs: Responses

Any individual observing violent or threatening behavior that poses an immediate danger to persons or property is expected to:

- Call 9-1-1 or Federal Protective Service 1-877-437-7411, or other appropriate emergency contacts for the facility, particularly if events occur that require medical and/or law enforcement assistance. Contact FEMA Office of the Chief Security Officer, Internal Investigation Branch at 1-866-847-7056 as soon as possible.
- Secure your personal safety first—leave the area if safety is at risk.
- Remain calm and contact the supervisor.
- Contact other people who may be in danger. Keep emergency numbers for employees up to date and accessible.
- Cooperate with law enforcement personnel when they have responded to the situation. Be prepared to provide a description of the violent or threatening individual, details of what was observed, and the exact location of the incident.

Supervisors: Extreme Misconduct

In the case of extreme misconduct, such as acts of violence, supervisors should intervene quickly to investigate and take appropriate disciplinary/adverse action, **with assistance from the Crisis Management Team**. Appropriate action shall be taken:

- When standards of conduct are violated,
- When the employee's job performance or the job performance of others is affected, or
- When the mission of FEMA and the efficiency of service are affected.

In offices with no security or employee relations staff, the supervisor should consult with the staff by phone.

Supervisors: Signs of Violence Intervention Techniques

When an employee exhibits signs of violence and the situation is not life threatening, defuse the anger by using the following techniques:

- Meet with the employee in private to discuss the inappropriate behavior. Build trust by listening and treating the employee with respect.
- Do not argue, get defensive, or be sarcastic.
- Take all threats or acts of violence seriously.
- Counsel the employee about the misconduct and how it affects the work of other employees, with a specific warning on future disciplinary action if behavior continues.

If you are unable to defuse the situation and the threat of violence persists:

- Remain calm and do not put yourself or any staff member in a position to be injured.
- If you are meeting alone with the employee, ask the employee to remain and excuse yourself from the meeting.
- Call the appropriate officials for assistance as outlined in the Crisis Management Plan.
- After the situation has calmed down, counsel the employee in writing on the effect of the violent behavior and initiate appropriate disciplinary action based on the misconduct and/or disruption.

Supervisors: If Violence Occurs

Sometimes, despite everyone's best efforts to defuse a situation, actual violence occurs. If this happens, remain calm and do not put yourself or any staff member in a position to be injured.

You should call the appropriate officials for assistance as outlined in the Crisis Management Plan. Once the danger has passed, take appropriate disciplinary action.

Supervisors: Disciplinary Action for Extreme Misconduct

In cases of extreme misconduct, the supervisor and the Crisis Management Team meet with the employee and advise him or her that the conduct is unacceptable and access to the building has been restricted until further notice. The employee is escorted from the building by security, and keys and ID are confiscated.

The employee may be placed on administrative leave (paid non-duty status) until it is decided what, if any, action will be taken against the employee.

An inquiry or investigation is conducted to determine whether further action is warranted, such as a proposed suspension or removal, or some lesser action as appropriate.

Supervisors: Disciplinary Action for Lesser Forms of Misconduct

For lesser forms of misconduct, a first offense may result in counseling between the supervisor and employee, as well as a verbal or written warning.

In the case of a second lesser form offense, a letter of reprimand may be placed in the employee's Official Personnel Folder. A third offense may result in a proposed suspension or proposed removal, as determined appropriate.

Written warnings, reprimands, proposal notices, and decision notices must be coordinated with the Employee and Labor Relations Division and Office of Chief Counsel prior to issuance to an employee.

Prevention of Workplace Violence

This section deals with ways to help prevent Workplace Violence before it can ever occur.

Prevention of Workplace Violence: Environment

The best prevention strategy is to maintain an environment that minimizes negative feelings, such as isolation, resentment, and hostility among employees.

Although no workplace can be perceived as perfect by every employee, management can help create a professional, healthy, and caring work environment.

Some steps that management can take include:

- Promote sincere, open, and timely communication among managers, employees, and union representatives.
- Offer opportunities for professional development.
- Foster a family-friendly work environment.
- Maintain mechanisms for complaints and concerns and allow them to be expressed in a nonjudgmental forum that includes timely feedback to the initiator.
- Promote "quality of life" issues such as pleasant facilities and job satisfaction.

- Maintain impartial and consistent discipline for employees who exhibit improper conduct and poor performance.

Prevention of Workplace Violence: Security

FEMA uses a variety of security measures to help ensure a secure environment. Maintaining a secure and physically safe workplace is part of any good strategy for preventing workplace violence. The measures used depend on the resources available in the area, but can include:

- Employee photo identification badges.
- Onsite guard services.
- Guard force assistance in registering and directing visitors in larger facilities.
- Onsite law enforcement support to respond to requests for assistance.
- Other appropriate security measures (e.g., metal detectors).

Employees should notify the appropriate security office or designated police about suspicious or unauthorized individuals on Agency property.

Additional law enforcement assistance is available through local police departments for emergency situations.

Prevention of Workplace Violence: Education

Education and communication are also critical components of any prevention strategy. In addition to workplace violence training such as this course, educational offerings on the following topics may be useful:

- Communications
- Conflict resolution
- Anger management
- Stress reduction

Prevention of Workplace Violence: Observations

Be aware of performance and/or conduct problems that may be warning signs. Such signs may be present in perpetrators of violence, those who are victims, and those involved in domestic violence.

Though these indicators may occur in isolation, it is more likely that a pattern will appear or that they will represent a change from normal behavior. The presence of any of these characteristics does not necessarily mean a violent act will occur. They may be indicators of another type of problem such as being ill, depressed, or bereaved.

Observations: Performance Indicators

Examples of performance indicators include:

- **Attendance problems,** such as excessive sick leave, excessive tardiness, leaving work early, or improbable excuses for absences.
- **Decreased productivity,** including making excessive mistakes, using poor judgment, missing deadlines, or wasting work time or materials.

- **Inconsistent work patterns**, such as alternating periods of high/low productivity or quality of work, exhibiting inappropriate reactions, overreacting to criticism, or mood swings.
- **Concentration problems**, including becoming easily distracted or having difficulty recalling instructions, project details, or deadline requirements.
- **Adverse effect on supervisor's time** when he or she must spend an inordinate amount of time coaching and/or counseling the employee about personal problems, redoing the employee's work, or dealing with coworker concerns.

Observations: Behavioral Indicators

Examples of behavioral indicators include:

- **Continual excuses and blaming**, such as an inability to accept responsibility for even the most inconsequential errors.
- **Safety issues**, including a disregard for personal, equipment, and machinery safety or taking needless risks.
- **Unshakable depression**, as exhibited by low energy, little enthusiasm, and/or despair.
- **Evidence of serious stress** in the employee's personal life, such as crying, excessive personal phone calls, or recent change in family/relationship status.
- **Unusual or changed behavior**, such as:
  - Inappropriate comments, threats, throwing objects, etc.
  - Evidence of possible drug or alcohol use/abuse.
  - Poor health and hygiene (marked changes in personal grooming habits).

Prevention of Workplace Violence: Support Services

There are many avenues and types of support services available for employees to prevent Workplace Violence. Some forms of prevention include training, stress management programs, and enhanced communication by management team and with other employees, security personnel, stress managers and health professionals, and union representatives.

The **Alternative Dispute Resolution (ADR) Office** offers services and training to enhance communication and address conflict in the workplace in useful, creative, and nonadversarial ways. ADR Advisors possess extensive training and experience as third-party neutral facilitators. ADR services are voluntary and generally confidential and include conflict coaching, mediation, assessments, team building, and facilitated discussions. ADR Advisors do not provide short-term counseling or referrals in connection with alcohol/substance abuse, stress, grief, family problems, and psychological concerns. ADR Advisors may, however, upon request, provide information about local service providers.

Summary

This course described how to recognize the warning signs of Workplace Violence, and what actions to take to prevent or minimize violence. You should now be able to:

- Define Workplace Violence in accordance with the FEMA 121-7 Directive and the DHS memo referenced in the course.
- List the four types of Workplace Violence.
- Identify the three warning sign levels related to potential Workplace Violence.
- List the action steps taken in response to Workplace Violence.
- Identify ways to prevent Workplace Violence.

- For additional training on this subject area, please refer to IS-906 Workplace Security Awareness and IS-907 Active Shooter: What You Can Do.

Workplace Violence

Awareness and Prevention for Employers and Employees

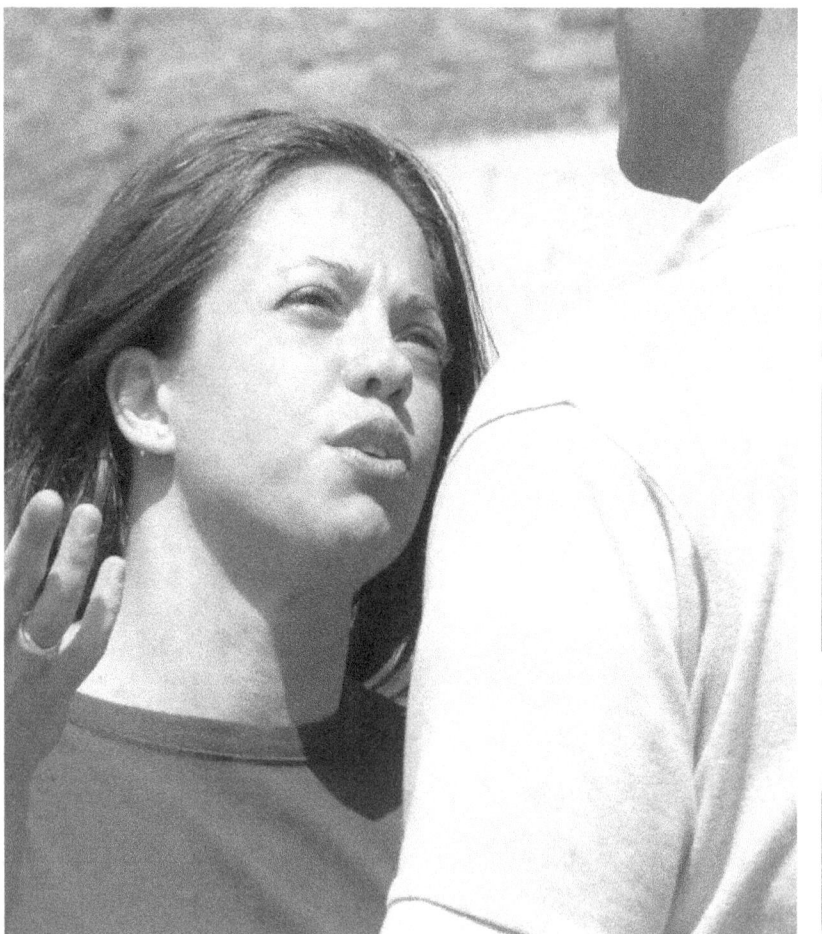

Division of Occupational Safety and Health

 www.Lni.wa.gov/Safety 1-800-423-7233

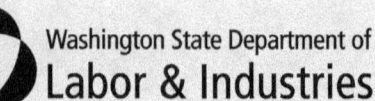
Washington State Department of
Labor & Industries

Workplace Violence

*Awareness and Prevention
for Employers and Employees*

Prepared by the Washington State
Department of Labor & Industries
Division of Occupational Safety and Health

Notice

This guidebook is meant to help employers and employees recognize workplace violence, minimize and prevent it, and respond appropriately if it occurs. Included in this guidebook is a sample workplace violence prevention program that employers can adapt to their company's size and type. The sample program can be incorporated into a company's accident prevention program, used to create a separate workplace violence prevention program, or included as part of an employee handbook.

Contents

1   **Overview**

Workplace Violence Defined

Costs of Workplace Violence

High-risk Industries

4   **Types of Workplace Violence and Their Characteristics**

Type 1: Violence by Strangers

Type 2: Violence by Customers or Clients

Type 3: Violence by Co-workers

Type 4: Violence by Personal Relations

6   **Violent Incidents: Case Scenarios, Potential Risk Factors and Potential Prevention Measures**

12   **Elements of a Workplace Violence Prevention Program**

14   **Responding If An Assault Occurs**

Appendixes

A Sample Workplace Violence Prevention Program

B Sample Forms

C Sample Training Techniques

D Sample Policy on Domestic Violence in the Workplace

E Selected Laws and Regulations

F Other Resources on Workplace Violence

G Technical Assistance and Training

Workplace violence can happen anywhere at any time. It can involve a single victim, such as the apartment manager stabbed to death in Everett in July 2010. It can involve multiple victims, as in the shooting at the Jewish Federation of Greater Seattle, when a gunman shot six workers, killing one, in July 2006.

News media accounts of these shootings, assaults, and other acts of violence at the workplace have heightened awareness of this problem.

Workers in some industries, such as health care or retail establishments, are more likely than others to experience violence on the job. For that reason, Washington State has laws that require workplace violence prevention programs in health care settings, psychiatric hospitals and late night retail establishments, like convenience stores.

You can find out more about these safety rules for workers in these industries in Appendix E.

Regardless of whether your worksite falls within these rules, however, every business should consider establishing a workplace violence prevention plan.

Such a plan does not have to be complicated, time consuming or expensive. Ask yourself, "What kind of workplace violence could happen at my work?" Then use this guide and the tips included to plan ways to reduce the possibility of violence at work.

Violence is the second leading cause of work-related death for women in the United States.

Workplace violence causes a significant number of fatalities and injuries in Washington and throughout the United States. The Bureau of Labor Statistics' Census of Fatal Occupational Injuries (CFOI) reports that homicides due to workplace violence are the fourth-leading cause of work-related deaths. For women, violence is the second leading cause of workplace fatalities in the United States.

Bureau of Labor Statistics (BLS) data for 2009 showed violence as the second-leading cause of workplace deaths in Washington State. Transportation accidents, being "struck by" equipment or objects and falls accounted for most other workplace fatalities. In addition, in 2009 Washington State experienced its highest number of workplace violence-related deaths in more than a decade. Of 62 work-related fatalities, 13 were on-the-job homicides and seven were suicides.

Nationally, non-fatal acts of violence in the workplace are numerous. In 2009, approximately 572,000 non-fatal violent crimes (rape/sexual assault, robbery, and aggravated and simple assault) occurred against workers, according to data from the National Crime Victimization Survey.

There is a strong association between violence in the home or community, and violence in the workplace. For example, BLS data from 1997–2009 show that 381 women killed in the workplace were murdered by a husband, male partner, or other relative or acquaintance.

Employers can take steps to make the workplace safer. It is critical that business, labor, social and health services, education, law enforcement and government undertake a collaborative approach to prevention.

Cost of Workplace Violence

Workplace violence is any verbal assault, threatening behavior, or physical assault occurring in or arising from the worksite.

Shootings, assaults, and other incidents of workplace violence routinely make the news. Recent media coverage has included a 39-year-old King County taxi driver on the way to pick up a passenger who was shot in the head; a 55-year-old self-employed tool salesman who was robbed and murdered in Pierce County en-route to a delivery; a 35-year-old business owner shot and killed by her estranged husband in her Clallam County office; and a 44-year-old middle school teacher in Benton County returning a video to school late in the evening assaulted in the hallway of the school.

Workplace violence injures and kills real people and affects victims' families, friends and co-workers. While the human costs of workplace violence cannot be calculated, many of the financial impacts can be estimated. For non-fatal injuries related to assaults and violence, the BLS estimates there are an annual average of nearly 800 lost workday assault-related injuries in Washington State. Here are a few other striking facts:

- Workers' compensation data for both the State fund and self-insured employers show an average of more than 2,000 claims related to assaults and violence each year, an amount equal to 12 such claims per 10,000 full time workers.

- The National Safe Workplace Institute estimates that costs to employers in missed days of work and legal expenses exceed $4 billion annually.

- Employers also may incur replacement and/or retraining costs; lost production costs; administrative costs and potential litigation costs. Such "indirect" costs are highly variable, but are commonly suggested to be 1.5 to 2 times the direct costs of medical treatment, wage-replacement and disability pensions.

High-risk Industries

A review of workplace violence data reveals that some types of violence are not random, but for the most part occur predictably in certain types of workplaces or occupations. Violence prevention efforts are especially important for these "high risk" industries and occupations.

In Washington State, the industries at highest risk of workplace violence include:

- Health care
- Social services
- Security services
- Public administration
- Education
- Law enforcement
- Retail trade
- Public transportation
- Accommodation and food services

These industries are similar to those identified as high risk in the national data.

By law, all employers in Washington State must provide a workplace free from recognized hazards. At any worksite where workplace violence is determined to be a hazard, a workplace violence prevention plan would be required.

But incidents of workplace violence can happen anywhere. For this reason, all employers should take steps to prevent or reduce the risk of workplace violence.

Types of Workplace Violence and Their Characteristics

Workplace violence takes several forms, including verbal threats, threatening behavior or physical assaults. It can be classified as to "type" depending on the relationship of the assailant to the worker or the workplace. Their specific characteristics are described below.

Type 1: Violence by Strangers

This is violence committed by an assailant who has no legitimate business relationship to the workplace or the worker. For example, the person enters the workplace to commit a robbery or other criminal act. In Washington State, violence by strangers accounts for most of the fatalities related to workplace violence. Workplaces at risk of violence by strangers commonly include late night retail establishments and taxi cabs.

Type 2: Violence by Customers or Clients

This is violence committed by an assailant who either receives services from or is under the custodial supervision of the affected workplace or the victim. Assailants can be current or former customers or clients such as passengers, patients, students, inmates, criminal suspects or prisoners. The workers typically provide direct services to the public, for example, municipal bus or railway drivers, health care and social service providers, teachers and sales personnel. Law enforcement personnel are also at risk of assault from individuals over whom they exert custodial supervision. Violence by customers or clients may occur on a daily basis in certain industries; they represent the majority of non-fatal injuries related to workplace violence in Washington State.

Type 3: Violence by Co-workers

This involves violence by an assailant who has some employment-related involvement with the workplace, for example, a current or former employee, supervisor or manager. Any workplace can be at risk of violence by a co-worker. In committing a threat or assault, the individual may be seeking revenge for what is perceived as unfair treatment.

Fatalities related to violence by co-workers have received much media attention, but account for only a small proportion of all workplace violence related fatalities. Strangers cause most workplace violence fatalities.

Type 4: Violence by Personal Relations

This includes incidents of domestic violence at the workplace by an assailant who confronts an individual with whom he or she has or had a personal relationship outside of work. Personal relations include a current or former spouse, lover, relative, friend or acquaintance. The assailant's actions are motivated by perceived difficulties in the relationship or by psycho-social factors that are specific to the assailant.

Violent Incidents:
Case Scenarios, Potential Risk Factors and Potential Prevention Measures

The types of violence identified in the previous section illustrate different characteristics of workplace violence and the ways violence may present itself. The significance of these four types is that each involves somewhat different risk factors and means of preventing or responding to the potential violent incident.

> "A risk factor is a condition or circumstance that may increase the likelihood of violence..."

A risk factor is a condition or circumstance that may increase the likelihood of violence occurring in a particular setting. For instance, handling money in a retail service makes that workplace a more likely target for robbery, the most common kind of violence by strangers in the workplace. An attorney's office, where all payments are received by check and money is not directly handled, would not present the same kind of target and would not be at the same degree of risk of violence due to the handling of money.

Different risk factors might predominate in the attorney's office. An attorney might be working in the office late at night after business hours. He or she might be subject to violence from a customer or client who is dissatisfied with the outcome of litigation. In this example, several risk factors are combined, increasing the overall risk to the attorney.

Each risk factor only represents a potential for an increased likelihood of violence. No risk factor, or combination of risk factors, guarantees that violence will occur or that its incidence will increase. However, the presence of these risk factors, particularly of several in combination, increases the likelihood that violence will occur.

The following general factors, which may have the potential to increase an employee's risk for workplace violence, have been identified in various studies.

General risk factors include:

- Contact with the public.
- Exchange of money.
- Delivery of passengers, goods, or services.
- Having a mobile workplace such as a taxicab or police cruiser.
- Working with unstable or volatile persons in health care, social services, or criminal justice settings.
- Working in isolation.
- Working late at night or during early morning hours.
- Working in high-crime areas.
- Guarding valuable property or possessions.
- Working in community-based settings.

Some risk factors are more likely to pertain to one or more of the four types of violence in the workplace. The following case scenarios illustrate the four types of violence. Potential risk factors for each case (you may be able to identify others), and examples of potential prevention measures pertaining to those risk factors are listed. Keep in mind that specific prevention techniques will vary according to circumstances and resources available.

The case scenarios are designed to help you think about your company's potential risk factors. It is up to you to think through those that might affect you and your personnel. From there, you can determine how best to mitigate those risks using prevention measures designed to work within your resources and in your unique workplace.

Violence by Strangers (Type 1)

It's 1 a.m. and a man enters a grocery store. He goes to a cooler, gets a six-pack of beer and heads to the checkout stand. When the clerk rings up the sale, the man pulls out a gun and tells the clerk to open the till. As the robber starts grabbing the cash from the till, a customer enters the store. The frightened clerk sees this as an opportunity to thwart the robbery, and shoves the cash register drawer onto the robber's hand. The surprised robber fires his gun repeatedly, hitting both the clerk and the customer before fleeing the store.

Potential Risk Factors

- Working with money
- Working alone
- Working late at night
- Isolated worksite
- Poor visibility into worksite
- Poor lighting outside of worksite
- High crime area

Potential Prevention Measures

To identify the prevention measures needed in your organization, first conduct a hazard assessment. A comprehensive workplace violence program could include measures such as the following:

- Training (include de-escalation techniques appropriate to your industry)
- Post signs stating cash register only contains minimal cash
- Leave a clear, unobstructed view of cash register from street
- Have a drop safe, limited access safe or comparable device
- Address adequate outside lighting
- Examine and address employee isolation factors
- Provide security personnel
- Communication method to alert police/security
- Increase police patrol in the area
- Post laws against assault, stalking or other violent acts

Violence by Customers or Clients (Type 2)

Mary is a social worker in a child welfare office. Her office space is a cubicle with one entry. One night, Mary was working late after most of her co-workers had left. The mother of one of her clients walked into her cubicle unannounced. She was quite emotional, and had a history of being verbally assaultive and threatening. Mary asked her to leave and make an appointment to see her the next day. The mother said she wanted her child back immediately and picked up a pair of scissors on Mary's desk. Mary asked for the scissors back, and when the mother refused, Mary picked up the phone to dial security. While Mary was calling security, the mother stabbed Mary's hand and ripped the phone out of the socket.

Potential Risk Factors

- Working in isolation
- Working after regular work hours
- Lack of controlled access to worksite
- Dealing with customers with past violent behavior
- Potential weapons[1] (such as scissors) easily visible and accessible
- Lack of a quick communication mechanism to security personnel
- Lack of alternate escape route

Potential Prevention Measures

To identify the prevention measures needed in your organization, first conduct a hazard assessment. A comprehensive workplace violence program could include measures such as the following:

- Training (including de-escalation techniques appropriate to your industry)
- Control access to worksite (e.g., posted restricted access, locked doors)
- Examine and address employee isolation factors
- Quick communication method to alert security
- Eliminate easy access to potential weapons
- Client referral/assistance programs
- Set up worksite so employees are not trapped from exiting
- Provide security personnel
- Post laws against assault, stalking or other violent acts

---

1. A weapon is any physical object that can be used to inflict injury or cause death.

Violence by Co-Workers (Type 3)

Bob supervises 14 workers at a small warehouse operated by Company X. The warehouse may be making layoffs soon; all the workers, including Bob, are concerned about their jobs. Company X management says it will make a decision within six months, but also says that productivity will have to increase substantially to keep the warehouse open. Bob starts disciplining workers he thinks are not working productively. When he meets with one worker, Doug, and informs him that he will be disciplined for poor work performance, Doug becomes angry and starts to shout at Bob. A week later, Bob suspends Doug for a week for continuing aggressive, threatening behavior. At that point, Doug pushes Bob away from him and the two men get into a fistfight.

Potential Risk Factors

- High stress in the workplace (impending layoffs, for example) and outside, non-work related stress
- Lack of appropriate management protocols for disciplinary actions
- Individual with a history of violent behavior
- Lack of appropriate training for supervisors

Potential Prevention Measures

To identify the prevention measures needed in your organization, first conduct a hazard assessment. A comprehensive workplace violence program could include measures such as the following:

- Training (including de-escalation techniques appropriate to your industry)
- Enforced policy on no tolerance for workplace violence
- Management strategy for layoffs
- Management policy for disciplinary actions
- Access to employee assistance program or other counseling services
- Policy prohibiting weapons
- Provide security personnel
- Post laws against assault, stalking or other violent acts

Violence by Personal Relations (Type 4)

Sue, a secretary at the local high school, went through a difficult divorce last year. Her ex-husband, Tod, did not want the divorce. Tod has called Sue regularly asking to reconcile and he has begun coming by her office to leave messages and gifts. Sue has asked him not to call or come by the school. One of her co-workers suggested that she seek a restraining order against Tod, but Sue felt she could handle it on her own. Finally, Tod leaves Sue a message that he doesn't want to live unless he can reconcile with her. Sue calls him back and urges him to see a therapist but refuses to meet or talk with him. On the anniversary of their divorce, Tod goes to the high school and waits for Sue in the lobby. When Sue approaches the lobby, he rushes toward her with a gun, shoots her, then shoots himself.

Potential Risk Factors

- Individual with history of violent/threatening behavior
- Lack of controlled access to the worksite
- No communication policy regarding restraining orders
- Domestic violence

Potential Prevention Measures

To identify the prevention measures needed in your organization, first conduct a hazard assessment. A comprehensive workplace violence program could include measures such as the following:

- Domestic violence training (including de-escalation techniques)
- Enforced policies on handling/preventing violence situations
- Restraining orders
- Control access to worksite
- Access to consultation with employer, employee assistance program or other counseling program
- Enforced policy prohibiting weapons
- Reporting procedures
- Relocating within worksite where possible
- Necessary staff notification
- Provide security personnel
- Post laws against assault, stalking or other violent acts

Elements of a Workplace Violence Prevention Program

As noted by many professionals working on the workplace violence issue, violent acts generally occur in predictable types of worksites or settings, are associated with identifiable risk factors, and may be eliminated or controlled through effective prevention strategies. (See Appendix A for a sample workplace violence prevention program.) Programs to prevent workplace violence, just like other workplace hazard prevention programs, often include the following key elements:

MANAGEMENT COMMITMENT & EMPLOYEE INVOLVEMENT

To ensure an effective program, managers and employees should work together, perhaps through a team approach, to provide the motivation, commitment of resources, and feedback to address workplace violence issues.

HAZARD ASSESSMENT

Hazard assessment involves a step-by-step, common sense look at the workplace to find existing or potential hazards for workplace violence. This can include:

- Analyzing and tracking records of violence at work.
- Examining specific violence incidents carefully.
- Surveying employees to gather their ideas and input.
- Periodic inspections of the worksite to identify risk factors that could contribute to injuries related to violence.

The hazard assessment should examine vulnerability to the four categories of violence previously described — violence by strangers, violence by customers or clients, violence by co-workers, and violence by personal relations.

HAZARD PREVENTION AND CONTROL

Once existing or potential hazards are identified through the hazard assessment, then hazard prevention and control measures can be identified and implemented.

These measures may include (in order of general preference):

- Engineering controls, such as locks and alarms.
- Administrative/work practice controls, such as sign-in procedures for visitors and employee assistance programs.
- Personal protective equipment, such as bullet-proof vests for police and security personnel.
- Posting applicable laws, such as those prohibiting assaults and stalking, in visible locations may serve as a prevention measure.

TRAINING AND INSTRUCTION

Training and instruction on workplace violence ensures that all staff are aware of potential hazards and how to protect themselves and their co-workers through established prevention and control measures.

REPORTING PROCEDURE

A reporting procedure for violent incidents should be developed for all types of violent incidents, whether or not physical injury has occurred. Violence other than physical injury would include, for example, verbal abuse or threats of violence. This procedure should be in writing and should be easily understood by all employees. It should take into account issues of confidentiality. Employees may be reluctant to come forward otherwise and they should not fear reprisal for bringing their concerns to management's attention.

RECORD KEEPING

Record keeping is essential to the success of a workplace violence prevention program. Good records help employers determine the severity of the problem, evaluate methods of hazard control, and identify training needs.

EVALUATION

As part of an overall program covering workplace violence, employers should evaluate their safety and security measures. Management should share the evaluation results with all employees. Any changes in the program should be discussed at regular meetings of the safety committee, with union representatives or other employee groups.

Responding If An Assault Occurs

Employers should prepare a plan that outlines the steps to take if an assault occurs. What are the priorities?

Immediately after an assault occurs, an employer should focus first on the medical and psychological needs of affected employees. Other immediate steps include:

1. Call the police and help them in their work, for example by providing access to the crime scene for their investigation, assisting them in locating witnesses, victims and others to interview.
2. Secure work areas where disturbances occurred.
3. As soon as possible, account for all your workers and others in the area and make sure they are safe.
4. Provide for site security and ensure that no work area is left short-staffed while others assist the victim or help in securing the area.
5. Quickly assess the work area if it was disturbed or damaged during an incident and determine if it is safe.
6. Talk to victims, witnesses, and other affected employees in confidence. Allow them to express their feelings and encourage them to seek treatment if appropriate.
7. Provide accurate communication to outside agencies, media and law enforcement.

Additional attention to employees' medical and psychological needs may be necessary. Employees may need the services of an employee assistance program or other counseling services. Provisions for follow-up after medical and psychological treatment, medical confidentiality, and protection from discrimination must be addressed to prevent the victims of workplace violence from suffering further loss.

Investigation and Evaluation

After an incident occurs, a detailed investigation by the company safety and health committee or the employer is imperative. All incidents, including near misses, should be investigated as soon as possible. A delay of any kind may cause important evidence to be removed or destroyed intentionally or unintentionally.

Important Records to Keep

- Log of injuries and illnesses (OSHA).

- Medical reports of worker injury; reports for each recorded assault.

- Incidents of assault and threats of violence. (See sample forms in Appendix B.)

- Information on high-risk clients with a history of past violence. (Share with employees who need to know.)

- Minutes of safety meetings.

- Records of hazard analyses and corrective actions recommended.

- Records of relevant training conducted, attendees and qualification of trainers.

The investigation should focus on determining the facts of what happened to prevent it from happening again, and not finding fault with anyone. Employers should maintain comprehensive records of the investigation. (See Appendix B, Assault Incident Report Form.)

When conducting the investigation:

- Collect facts on who, what, when, where and how the incident occurred.

- Get statements from witnesses and take photos of the damage or injuries where appropriate.

- Identify contributing causes.

- Recommend corrective action.

- Encourage appropriate follow-up.

- Consider changes in controls, procedures or policies.

After an incident occurs, it is especially important to review the workplace violence prevention program and assess its effectiveness. Identify any deficiencies and correct them.

Steps in the Evaluation Process

- Create a violence reporting system.

- Regularly review your workplace violence reports and logs. (See Appendix B.)

- Ask your employees for input on safety and security problems. (See Appendix B for sample survey.)

- Track changes in engineering controls and administrative and work practices designed to prevent workplace violence.

- Analyze trends in workplace violence-related injuries relative to "baseline" rates.

- Keep up on the latest strategies to deal with violence.

- Measure improvement based on lowering the frequency and severity of workplace violence.

SAMPLE Workplace Violence Prevention Program

An employer may choose to create a separate workplace violence prevention program or incorporate this information into other company documents: for example, the company's accident prevention program or an employee handbook.

Policy Statement *(Effective Date of Program)*

Our establishment, *[Employer Name]* is concerned and committed to our employees' safety and health. We refuse to tolerate violence in the workplace and will make every effort to prevent violent incidents from occurring by implementing a Workplace Violence Prevention Program (WVPP). We will provide adequate authority and budgetary resources to responsible parties so that our goals and responsibilities can be met.

All managers, supervisors and employees are responsible for implementing and maintaining our WVPP. We encourage employee participation in designing and implementing our program. We require prompt and accurate reporting of all violent incidents whether or not physical injury has occurred. We will not discriminate against victims of workplace violence.

A copy of this policy statement and our WVPP is readily available to all employees and from each manager and supervisor.

Our program ensures that all employees, including supervisors and managers, adhere to work practices that are designed to make the workplace more secure, and do not engage in verbal threats or physical actions which create a security hazard for others in the workplace.

All employees, including managers and supervisors, are responsible for using safe work practices, for following all directives, policies and procedures, and for assisting in maintaining a safe and secure work environment.

The management of our establishment is responsible for ensuring that all safety and health policies and procedures involving workplace security are clearly communicated and understood by all employees. Managers and supervisors are expected to enforce the rules fairly and uniformly.

Our program will be reviewed and updated annually.

Responsibility

The Workplace Violence Prevention Program Administrator is *[Program Administrator]* and *[he/she]* has the authority and responsibility for implementing the provisions of this program for *[Establishment Name]*. All managers, supervisors and employees are responsible for implementing and maintaining the WVPP in their work areas and for answering employee questions about the program.

In addition, a Workplace Violence Prevention Group will be established to assess the vulnerability to workplace violence at our establishment and reach agreement on preventive actions to be taken. This group will be responsible for developing employee-training programs in violence prevention and plans for responding to acts of violence. They will also audit our overall Workplace Violence Prevention Program.

The Workplace Violence Prevention Group will consist of:

Name: _____ Title: _____ Phone: _____

Name: _____ Title: _____ Phone: _____

Name: _____ Title: _____ Phone: _____

Name: _____ Title: _____ Phone: _____

Name: _____ Title: _____ Phone: _____

Compliance

We have established the following policy to ensure compliance with our rules on workplace security.

Management of our establishment is committed to ensuring that all safety and health policies and procedures involving workplace security are clearly communicated and understood by employees. All employees are responsible for using safe work practices, for following all directives, policies and procedures, and for assisting in maintaining a safe and secure work environment.

Our system ensures that all employees, including supervisors and managers, comply with work practices that are designed to make the workplace more secure, and do not engage in threats or physical actions which create a security hazard for others in the workplace. It includes:

☐ Informing employees, supervisors and managers about our Workplace Violence Prevention Program.

☐ Evaluating the performance of all employees in complying with our establishment's workplace security measures.

☐ Recognizing employees who perform work practices which promote security in the workplace.

☐ Providing training and/or counseling to employees who need to improve work practices designed to ensure workplace security.

☐ Disciplining employees for failure to comply with workplace security practices.

☐ The following practices that ensure employee compliance with workplace security directives, policies and procedures. *[Insert list specific to your worksite.]*

At our establishment, we recognize that to maintain a safe, healthy and secure workplace we must have open, two-way communication between all employees, including managers and supervisors, on all workplace safety, health and security issues. Our establishment has a communication system designed to encourage a continuous flow of safety, health and security information between management and our employees without fear of reprisal and in a form that is readily understandable. Our communication system consists of the following items:

☐ New employee orientation on our establishment's workplace security policies, procedures and work practices.

☐ Periodic review of our Workplace Violence Prevention Program with all personnel.

☐ Training programs designed to address specific aspects of workplace security unique to our establishment.

☐ Regularly scheduled safety meetings with all personnel that include workplace security discussions.

☐ A system to ensure that all employees, including managers and supervisors, understand the workplace security policies.

☐ Posted or distributed workplace security information.

☐ A system for employees to inform management about workplace security hazards or threats of violence.

☐ Procedures for protecting employees who report threats from retaliation by the person making the threats.

☐ Our establishment has fewer than ten employees and communicates with and instructs employees orally about general safe work practices with respect to workplace security.

☐ Other: _____

Hazard Assessment

The Workplace Violence Prevention Group will perform workplace hazard assessment for workplace security in the form of record keeping and review, periodic workplace security inspections, and a workplace survey. The assessment group will identify workplace violence and security issues and make recommendations to management and employees.

RECORD KEEPING AND REVIEW

Note: Care must be taken to ensure appropriate confidentiality of medical and personnel records, as required by WISHA (Washington Industrial Safety and Health Act), Department of Health, ADA (Americans with Disabilities Act) and other applicable regulations or policies.

Periodic updates and reviews of the following workplace violence reports and records will be made:

☐ Occupational Safety and Health Administration (OSHA) 300 logs

☐ Workplace violence incident reports

☐ Information compiled for recording assault incidents or near-assault incidents (i.e. Threat & Assault Log)

☐ Insurance records

☐ Police reports

☐ Workplace survey

☐ Accident investigations

☐ Training records

☐ Grievances

☐ Inspection information

☐ Other relevant records or information

The records review will be performed on the following schedule: _____.

WORKPLACE SECURITY INSPECTIONS

Periodic inspections to identify and evaluate workplace security hazards and threats of workplace violence will be performed by the following observer(s) in the following areas of our workplace:

Observer	Area

Periodic inspections are performed according to the following schedule:

☐ _____ (Frequency — weekly, monthly, etc.);

☐ When we initially established our Workplace Violence Prevention Program;

☐ When new, previously unidentified security hazards are recognized;

☐ When occupational injuries or threats of injury occur; and

☐ Whenever workplace security conditions warrant an inspection.

Periodic inspections for security hazards consist of identification and evaluation of workplace security hazards and changes in employee work practices, and may require assessing for more than one type of workplace violence. Our establishment performs inspections for each type of workplace violence by using the methods specified below to identify and evaluate workplace security hazards.

Inspections for workplace security hazards from violence by strangers (Type 1) include assessing:

☐ The exterior and interior of the workplace for its attractiveness to robbers.

☐ The need for security surveillance measures, such as mirrors or cameras.

☐ Posting of signs notifying the public that limited cash is kept on the premises.

☐ Procedures for employee response during a robbery or other criminal act.

☐ Procedures for reporting suspicious persons or activities.

☐ Posting of emergency telephone numbers for law enforcement, fire and medical services where employees have access to a telephone with an outside line.

☐ Limiting the amount of cash on hand and using time access safes for large bills.

☐ Staffing levels during evening hours of operation and at other high risk times.

☐ The use of work practices such as "buddy" systems, as appropriate, for identified risks (e.g., walking employees to their cars or mass transit stops at the end of the work day).

☐ Adequacy of lighting and security for designated parking lots or areas.

☐ Other: _____

Inspections for workplace security hazards from violence by customers or clients (Type 2) include assessing:

☐ Access to, and freedom of movement within, the workplace.

☐ Adequacy of workplace security systems, such as door locks, security windows, physical barriers and restraint systems.

☐ Frequency and severity of threatening or hostile situations that may lead to violent acts by persons who are service recipients of our establishment.

☐ Employees' skill in safely handling threatening or hostile service recipients.

☐ Effectiveness of systems and procedures to warn others of a security danger or to summon assistance, e.g. alarms or panic buttons.

☐ The use of work practices such as "buddy" systems, as appropriate, for identified risks (e.g., walking employees to their cars or mass transit stops at the end of the work day).

☐ Adequacy of lighting and security for designated parking lots or areas.

☐ The availability of employee escape routes.

☐ Other: _____

Inspections for workplace security hazards from violence by co-workers (Type 3) include assessing:

☐ How well our establishment's anti-violence policy has been communicated to employees, supervisors and managers.

☐ How well our establishment's management and employees communicate with each other.

☐ How well our employees, supervisors and managers know the warning signs of potential workplace violence.

☐ Access to, and freedom of movement within, the workplace by non-employees, specifically recently discharged employees.

☐ Frequency and severity of employee-reported threats of physical or verbal abuse by managers, supervisors or other employees.

☐ Any prior violent acts, threats of physical violence, verbal abuse, property damage or other signs of strain or pressure in the workplace.

☐ Employee disciplinary and discharge procedures.

☐ Other: _____

Inspection for workplace security hazards from violence by personal relations (Type 4) include assessing:

☐ Access to, and freedom of movement within, the workplace by non-employees, specifically personal relations with whom one of our employee's is having a dispute.

☐ Frequency and severity of employee-reported threats of physical or verbal abuse which may lead to violent acts by a personal relation.

☐ Adequacy of workplace security systems, such as door locks, security windows, and physical barriers.

☐ Any prior violent acts, threats of physical violence, verbal abuse, property damage or other signs.

☐ The use of work practices such as "buddy" systems, as appropriate, for identified risks (e.g., walking employees to their cars or mass transit stops at the end of the work day).

☐ Adequacy of lighting and security for designated parking lots or areas.

☐ Warnings or police involvement to remove personal relations of employees from the worksite and effectiveness of restraining orders.

WORKPLACE SURVEY

Under the direction of the Workplace Violence Prevention Administrator & Group, we distributed a survey among all of our employees to identify any additional issues that were not noted in the records review or the security inspection. (See sample survey, Appendix B.)

FINAL RECOMMENDATIONS

Based on the records review, workplace security inspections and workplace survey, the Workplace Violence Prevention Group has identified the following issues that need to be addressed:

_____

_____

_____

_____

_____

_____

Workplace Hazard Control and Prevention

In order to reduce the risk of workplace violence, the following measures have been recommended:

Engineering Controls and Building or Work Area Design:

_____

_____

_____

_____

Workplace Practices:

_____

_____

_____

Management has instituted the following as a result of the workplace violence hazard assessment and the recommendations made by the Workplace Violence Prevention Group:

_____

_____

_____

These changes were completed on *[date]*.

Policies and procedures developed as a result of the Workplace Violence Prevention Group's recommendations:

_____

_____

_____

Training and Instruction

We have established the following policy on training all employees with respect to workplace violence and security.

All employees, including managers and supervisors, shall have training and instruction on general and job-specific workplace security practices. Training and instruction shall be provided when the Workplace Violence Prevention Program is first established and periodically thereafter. Training shall be provided to all new employees and to other employees for whom training has not previously been provided. It shall also be provided to all employees, supervisors, and managers given new job assignments for which specific workplace security training for the job assignment has not previously been provided. Additional training and instruction will be provided to all personnel whenever the employer is made aware of new or previously unrecognized security hazards.

General workplace violence and security training and instruction includes, but is not limited to, the following:

☐ Explanation of the Workplace Violence Prevention Program including measures for reporting any violent acts or threats of violence.

☐ Recognition of workplace security hazards including the risk factors associated with the four types of violence.

☐ Measures to prevent workplace violence, including procedures for reporting workplace security hazards or threats to managers and supervisors.

☐ Ways to defuse hostile or threatening situations.

☐ Measures to summon others for assistance.

☐ Employee routes of escape.

☐ Notification of law enforcement authorities when a criminal act may have occurred.

☐ Emergency medical care provided in the event of any violent act upon an employee.

☐ Post-event trauma counseling for those employees desiring such assistance.

In addition, we provide specific instructions to all employees regarding workplace security hazards unique to their job assignment, to the extent that such information was not already covered in other training.

We have chosen the following items for training and instruction for managers, supervisors and employees:

- ☐ Crime awareness.
- ☐ Location and operation of alarm systems, panic buttons and other protective devices.
- ☐ Communication procedures.
- ☐ Proper work practices for specific workplace activities, occupations or assignments, such as late night retail sales, taxi-cab driver, security guard, law enforcement, health care, public transportation, etc.
- ☐ Self-protection.
- ☐ Dealing with angry, hostile or threatening individuals.
- ☐ Using the "buddy" system or other assistance from co-employees.
- ☐ Awareness of indicators that lead to violent acts by service recipients.
- ☐ Employee assistance programs.
- ☐ Review of anti-violence policy and procedures.
- ☐ Managing with respect and consideration for employee well-being.
- ☐ Pre-employment screening practices.
- ☐ Role playing a violent incident.

Incident Investigation

Our procedures for investigating incidents of workplace violence — threats and physical injury — include:

- ☐ Reviewing all previous incidents.
- ☐ Visiting the scene of an incident as soon as possible.
- ☐ Interviewing threatened or injured employees and witnesses.
- ☐ Examining the workplace for security risk factors associated with the incident, including any previous reports of inappropriate behavior by the perpetrator.
- ☐ Determining the cause of the incident.
- ☐ Taking corrective action to prevent the incident from recurring.
- ☐ Recording the findings and corrective actions taken.
- ☐ Other: _____

These sample forms may be useful to carry out or enhance your workplace violence program. They are not mandatory, and should be tailored to fit your organization's needs.

Sample Assault Incident Report Form

This type of form can be used to report any threatening remark or act of physical violence against a person or property, whether *experienced* or *observed*. Individuals may be more forthcoming with information if the form is understood to be voluntary and confidential. The form also needs to identify where it should be sent after completion (for example, workplace violence prevention group or safety committee representative).

Sample Threat and Assault Log

This type of log can help summarize and characterize reports of threats and assaults in your company over the course of a year. This information may prove helpful to your workplace violence prevention group (or administrator) when considering the need for additional hazard assessment, prevention measures or training.

Sample Employee Survey on Hazard Assessment

Periodically surveying employees on workplace violence can be a valuable tool for evaluating your workplace violence prevention efforts and gathering suggestions for improving your program. Some employees may prefer not to have their names identified on a survey; making the name "optional" may increase the amount of feedback you receive.

SAMPLE

Assault Incident Report Form · Page 1

Date of Incident	Year	Month	Day of Week

Location of Incident (map and sketch on reverse side)

Name of Victim	Gender: ☐ Male ☐ Female

Victim Description: ☐ Employee – Job Title _____ ☐ Client ☐ Visitor	Member of Labor Organization? ☐ Yes ☐ No

Assigned Work Location (if employee)

Supervisor	Has supervisor been notified? ☐ Yes ☐ No

Describe the assault incident.

List any witnesses to the incident (name and phone).

Did the assault involve a firearm? If so, describe.

Did the assault involve another weapon (not a firearm)? If so, describe.

Was the victim injured? If yes, please describe.

Who committed the assault?

Name (if known): _____

What is his/her status to the victim? ☐ Stranger ☐ Personal Relation ☐ Client / Patient / Customer
☐ Co-worker ☐ Supervisor ☐ Other: _____

What was the gender of the person(s) who committed the assault?

☐ Male ☐ Female

Assault Incident Report Form • Page 2

Please check any risk factors applicable to this incident. Each company should develop and include a list of potential risk factors that may apply in its worksite.

☐ Contact with the public.

☐ Working with money.

☐ Delivery of passengers, goods, or services.

☐ Having a mobile workplace such as a taxicab or police cruiser.

☐ Working with unstable or volatile persons in health care, social services, or criminal justice settings.

☐ Working in isolation.

☐ Working late at night or during early morning hours.

☐ Working in high-crime areas.

☐ Guarding valuable property or possessions.

☐ Working in community-based settings.

☐ Poor lighting outside of worksite.

☐ Other risk factor: _____

☐ Other risk factor: _____

What steps could be taken to avoid a similar incident in the future? (To avoid recreating trauma, sound judgment should be exercised in deciding when to request this information.)

Send completed form to: _____

SAMPLE

Threat and Assault Log | Year

Number of Threats and Assaults	January–June		July–December		Total	
	# Threats	# Assaults	# Threats	# Assaults	# Threats	# Assaults
Type of Threat or Assault	# Threats	# Assaults	# Threats	# Assaults	# Threats	# Assaults
Type 1 / Threat or assault by stranger						
Type 2 / Threat or assault by customers/clients						
Type 3 / Threat or assault by co-workers						
Type 4 / Threat or assault by personal relations						
Gender of Victims and Perpetrators	# Threats	# Assaults	# Threats	# Assaults	# Threats	# Assaults
Number of female victims						
Number of male victims						
Number of female perpetrators						
Number of male perpetrators						
Time of Threats and Assaults	# Threats	# Assaults	# Threats	# Assaults	# Threats	# Assaults
Day shift						
Evening shift						
Night shift						
On weekend						
Location of Threats and Assaults	# Threats	# Assaults	# Threats	# Assaults	# Threats	# Assaults
On work premises						
Parking lot						
Other duty station						
Other Considerations	# Threats	# Assaults	# Threats	# Assaults	# Threats	# Assaults
Threats and assaults involving firearms						
Threats and assaults involving other weapons (not firearms)						
Number of cases where the victim was working in isolation						
Result of Threats and Assaults						
Death						
Physical injury						
Stress/psychological impairment						
No injury						

SAMPLE

Employee Survey on Workplace Violence Hazard Assessment

Name (Optional) _____

Department/Unit _____ Date _____

Work Location (if at alternate worksite) _____

Please assess your department/unit over the last year. Circle TRUE (T), FALSE (F) or DON'T KNOW (?).
Thank you for your honest assessment.

				Management Commitment and Employee Involvement
T	F	?	1.	Violence/threats are not accepted as "part of the job" by managers, supervisors and/or employees.
T	F	?	2.	Employees communicate information about potentially assaultive/threatening clients or visitors to appropriate staff.
T	F	?	3.	Management communicates information to employees about incidents of workplace violence.
T	F	?	4.	Employees feel they are treated with dignity and respect by other employees and management.
T	F	?	5.	Employees are basically satisfied with their jobs.
T	F	?	6.	Employees are basically satisfied with management.
T	F	?	7.	Employees are basically satisfied with the organization (i.e., mission, vision, goals).
T	F	?	8.	Employees generally feel "safe" when they are at work.
T	F	?	9.	Employees are familiar with the department's/unit's violence prevention policy.

				Potential Risk Factors
T	F	?	10.	Employees do not work in high-crime areas.
T	F	?	11.	Employees do not work with drugs.
T	F	?	12.	Employees do not work with cash.
T	F	?	13.	Employees do not work with patients or clients who have a history of violent behavior or behavior disorders.
T	F	?	14.	Employees do not work in isolated work areas.

				Hazard Prevention and Control
T	F	?	15.	The department/unit has adequate lighting to, from and within the worksite.
T	F	?	16.	The employee parking garage is secure when arriving, leaving and during changes of shift.
T	F	?	17.	Access and freedom of movement within the workplace are restricted to those persons who have a legitimate reason for being there.
T	F	?	18.	Alarm systems such as panic alarm buttons, silent alarms, or personal electronic alarm systems are being used for prompt security assistance.
T	F	?	19.	Employees know to use security escort service after hours.

T	F	?	20.	After hours, the building is locked down with only one access point.
T	F	?	21.	Visitors are signed in and out.
T	F	?	22.	Exits are accessible and clearly marked.
T	F	?	23.	Employees are able to locate emergency equipment such as fire alarm boxes or emergency-generator outlets.
T	F	?	24.	Emergency equipment is accessible and free from obstruction.
T	F	?	25.	Employees are able to locate cellular phones, power-failure phones and/or radios for emergency communication.
T	F	?	26.	Employees know proper procedures if a bomb threat is announced.
T	F	?	27.	Employee emergency call-back list is up-to-date and available.
T	F	?	28.	Employees provide privacy to reflect sensitivity and respect for clients and visitors.
T	F	?	29.	Employees use the "buddy system" to work together if problems arise.
T	F	?	30.	Employees working in the field have cellular phones or other communication devices to enable them to request aid.
T	F	?	31.	Staffing levels are appropriate for department/unit functions.
T	F	?	32.	Reference manuals are up-to-date and available to employees.
T	F	?	33.	There is a grievance policy available to employees.
T	F	?	34.	There is a Safety Committee available as a resource to staff for any hazard concern.

			Training	
T	F	?	35.	Employees have received training on the company's workplace violence prevention program.
T	F	?	36.	Employees know how to ask for assistance by phone or by alerting other staff.
T	F	?	37.	Employees have been trained to recognize and handle threatening, aggressive, or violent behavior.
T	F	?	38.	Employees have been trained in verbal de-escalation techniques.
T	F	?	39.	Employees have been trained in self-defense/restraint procedures.

			Incidents and Reporting	
T	F	?	40.	This work unit/department has not experienced violent behavior and assaults or threats from strangers.
T	F	?	41.	This work unit/department has not experienced violent behavior and assaults or threats from clients or customers.
T	F	?	42.	This work unit/department has not experienced violent behavior and assaults or threats from others employed in the organization.
T	F	?	43.	This work unit/department has not experienced domestic violence issues.
T	F	?	44.	Employees are required to report incidents or threats of violence, regardless of injury or severity; the reporting system is clear.
T	F	?	45.	Medical and psychological counseling services were offered to employees who have been assaulted or threatened.

SAMPLE Training Techniques

Technique #1: Review Workplace Violence Prevention

Extent of the Problem

List statistics relative to your industry here. Use national and statewide information. You can also discuss the crime statistics of the neighborhood the company is in. Some of this information is available in the Overview Section at the beginning of this guidebook.

Risk Factors

Discuss the risk factors in your particular industry here. Look in the section titled "Violent Incidents: Case Scenarios, Potential Risk Factors and Potential Prevention Measures" in this guidebook.

Worksite Analysis

Discuss the violence history of your company. You can use the number of incidents, the rate and/or the types.

Security Hardware

Have the manager of your unit show you security hardware. (Put a checklist here of equipment you have at your company to prevent violence. This might include panic buttons, video cameras, security lighting, etc.)

_____

_____

_____

_____

Work Practice Controls

Discuss policies and procedures you have implemented to minimize violence in your company. Include any written procedures. Be sure to address your company's weapons policy and how to summon help in an emergency.

_____

_____

_____

_____

Follow Up Procedures

Report all assaults. (Include here a copy of the form your company uses to report violent incidents.)

File charges. *[Company name]* recommends that charges be filed in every case when an employee is assaulted. We will help you to do so including sending witnesses to testify if needed. No reprisals will be taken against any employee who is assaulted or files charges relating to an assault.

If a violent incident occurs, all affected staff will be offered counseling through an employee assistance program or other comparable counseling services.

Technique #2: Role Play Exercise to Defuse Violent Situations

Read the information in the charts below. Then have employees role play a confrontation. During the role play note the signs of escalating behavior and the techniques used to control it. Afterwards have the group discuss their observations. Address the following questions: What went well? What problems were there? What responses would work better?

Write a scenario about a violent incident for a couple of employees to act out. Use a case scenario in this guidebook or make up one appropriate to your company.

Technique #3: Hands-on Practice

If the violence in your workplace comes from unarmed people such as patients, you may want to train your employees in self defense and restraining techniques. Have your employees actually try out the techniques. Remember, in cases with armed perpetrators, such as robberies, it is usually safer to submit to the perpetrator's demands.

Five Warning Signs of Escalating Behavior

Confusion

Warning Signs	Possible Responses
Behavior characterized by bewilderment or distraction. Unsure or uncertain of the next course of action.	■ Listen to their concerns. ■ Ask clarifying questions. ■ Give them factual information.

Frustration

Warning Signs	Possible Responses
Behavior characterized by reaction or resistance to information. Impatience. Feeling a sense of defeat in the attempt of accomplishment. May try to bait you.	■ See steps above. ■ Relocate to quiet location or setting. ■ Reassure them. ■ Make a sincere attempt to clarify concerns.

Blame

Warning Signs	Possible Responses
Placing responsibility for problems on everyone else. Accusing or holding you responsible. Finding fault or error with the action of others. They may place blame directly on you. **Crossing over to potentially hazardous behavior.**	■ See steps above. ■ Disengage, bring second party into discussion. ■ Use teamwork approach. ■ Draw client back to facts. ■ Use probing questions. ■ Create "Yes" momentum.

Anger — Judgment call required

Warning Signs	Possible Responses
Characterized by a visible change in body posture and disposition. Actions include pounding fists, pointing fingers, shouting or screaming. **This signals very risky behavior.**	■ Utilize venting techniques. ■ Don't offer solutions. ■ Don't argue with comments made. ■ Prepare to evacuate or isolate. ■ Contact supervisor and/or security office.

Hostility — Judgment call required

Warning Signs	Possible Responses
Physical actions or threats which appear imminent. Acts of physical harm or property damage. Out-of-control behavior signals they have crossed over the line.	■ Disengage and evacuate. ■ Try to isolate person if it can be done safely. ■ Alert supervisor and contact security office immediately.

Personal Conduct to Minimize Violence*

Follow these suggestions in your daily interactions with people to de-escalate potentially violent situations. If at any time a person's behavior starts to escalate beyond your comfort zone, disengage.

Do	Do Not
■ Project calmness, move and speak slowly, quietly and confidently.	■ Use styles of communication which generate hostility such as apathy, brush off, coldness, condescension, robotism, going strictly by the rules or giving the run-around.
■ Be an empathetic listener: Encourage the person to talk and listen patiently.	
■ Focus your attention on the other person to let them know you are interested in what they have to say.	■ Reject all of a client's demands from the start.
■ Maintain a relaxed yet attentive posture and position yourself at a right angle rather than directly in front of the other person.	■ Pose in challenging stances such as standing directly opposite someone, hands on hips or crossing your arms. Avoid any physical contact, finger pointing or long periods of fixed eye contact.
■ Acknowledge the person's feelings. Indicate that you can see he/she is upset.	
■ Ask for small, specific favors such as asking the person to move to a quieter area.	■ Make sudden movements which can be seen as threatening. Notice the tone, volume and rate of your speech.
■ Establish ground rules if unreasonable behavior persists. Calmly describe the consequences of any violent behavior.	■ Challenge, threaten, or dare the individual. Never belittle the person or make him/her feel foolish.
■ Use delaying tactics which will give the person time to calm down. For example, offer a drink of water (in a disposable cup).	■ Criticize or act impatiently toward the agitated individual.
■ Be reassuring and point out choices. Break big problems into smaller, more manageable problems.	■ Attempt to bargain with a threatening individual.
■ Accept criticism in a positive way. When a complaint might be true, use statements like "You are probably right" or "It was my fault." If the criticism seems unwarranted, ask clarifying questions.	■ Try to make the situation seem less serious than it is.
	■ Make false statements or promises you cannot keep.
	■ Try to impart a lot of technical or complicated information when emotions are high.
■ Ask for his/her recommendations. Repeat back to him/her what you feel he/she is requesting of you.	■ Take sides or agree with distortions.
■ Arrange yourself so that a visitor cannot block your access to an exit.	■ Invade the individual's personal space. Make sure there is a space of three feet to six feet between you and the person.

*From *Combating Workplace Violence: Guidelines for Employers and Law Enforcement. International Association of Chiefs of Police. 1996.*

SAMPLE Policy on Domestic Violence in the Workplace

Description

Domestic violence is abusive behavior that is either physical, sexual, and/or psychological, intended to establish and maintain control over a partner. Domestic violence is a serious problem that affects people from all walks of life. It can adversely affect the well-being and productivity of employees who are victims, as well as their co-workers. Other effects of domestic violence in the workplace include increased absenteeism, turnover, health care costs, and reduced productivity.

Policy Statement

The *[Employer Name]* will not tolerate domestic violence including harassment of any employee or client while in our facilities, vehicles, on our property, or while conducting business. This includes the display of any violent or threatening behavior (verbal or physical) that may result in physical or emotional injury or otherwise places one's safety and productivity at risk.

Any employee who threatens, harasses, or abuses someone at our workplace or from the workplace using any company resources such as work time, workplace phones, FAX machines, mail, e-mail, or other means may be subject to corrective or disciplinary action, up to and including dismissal. Corrective or disciplinary action may also be taken against employees who are arrested, convicted or issued a permanent injunction as a result of domestic violence when such action has a direct connection to the employee's duties in our company.

The *[Employer Name]* is committed to working with employees who are victims of domestic violence to prevent abuse and harassment from occurring in the workplace. No employees will be penalized or disciplined solely for being a victim of harassment in the workplace. Our company will provide appropriate support and assistance to employees who are victims of domestic violence. This includes: confidential means for coming forward for help, resource and referral information, work schedule adjustments or leave as needed to obtain assistance, and workplace relocation as feasible.

Employees who are perpetrators of domestic violence are also encouraged to seek assistance. Our company will provide information regarding counseling and certified treatment resources, and make work schedule arrangements to receive such assistance.

Special Instructions for Employees

It is important that all employees know how best to respond to the effects of domestic violence in the workplace. In addition, they also should be aware of physical or behavioral changes in other employees and know who — personnel officer, manager, and or employee advisory service/resource — they can contact for advice. They should not attempt to diagnose the employee.

Managers/supervisors or human resource professionals in our company should receive domestic violence training. Our company should also:

- Be responsive when an employee who is either the victim or perpetrator of domestic violence asks for help.
- Maintain confidentiality. Information about the employee should only be given to others on a need-to-know basis.
- Work with the victim, personnel office, manager, employee advisory service/resource, available security staff, law enforcement, and community domestic violence programs, if necessary, to assess the need for and develop a workplace safety plan for the victim. Victims of domestic violence know their abusers better than anyone else. When it comes to their own personal safety, offer to assist them in developing a workplace safety plan, but allow them to decide what goes in it. If it is determined that other employees or clients are at risk, it is essential to take measures to provide protection for them.
- Adjust the employee's work schedule and/or grant leave if the employee needs to take time off for medical assistance, legal assistance, court appearances, counseling, relocation, or to make other necessary arrangements to create a safe situation. Be sure to follow all applicable personnel rules.
- Maintain communication with the employee during the employee's absence. Remember to maintain confidentiality of the employee's whereabouts.
- Post information about domestic violence in your work area. Also, have information available where employees can obtain it without having to request it or be seen removing it — such as rest rooms, lunchrooms, or where other employee resource information is located.
- Honor all civil protection orders. As appropriate, participate in court proceedings in obtaining protection orders on behalf of the employee.
- Maintain a list of services available to victims and perpetrators of domestic violence. This list should include: Employee Advisory Service/Resource, local shelters, certified domestic violence treatment programs available to perpetrators, information on how to obtain civil orders of protection, and any available community resources.
- Advise and assist supervisors and managers in taking corrective or disciplinary actions against perpetrators of domestic violence.

Options for Employees Who Are Victims of Domestic Violence

- Tell a trusted co-worker, supervisor, or manager, and ask for help.
- Contact your personnel officer for assistance.
- Contact the Employee Advisory Service/Resource.
- Contact the 24-hour Washington State Domestic Violence Hotline at 1-800-562-6025 (V/TTY).
- Call the local police.
- Notify your supervisor of the possible need to be absent. Find out what work schedule or leave options are available to you. Be clear about your plan to return to work and maintain communications with your supervisor during your absence.

- If appropriate and if safety is a concern, submit a recent photograph of the abuser and a copy of your protection order to your supervisor. This assists your employer in identifying the abuser should he/she appear in the workplace.

Options for Employees Who Are Perpetrators of Domestic Violence

- Tell a trusted co-worker, supervisor, or manager, and ask for help.
- Contact your personnel officer for assistance.
- Contact the Employee Advisory Service/Resource.
- Obtain a referral to a certified domestic violence perpetrators' treatment program.

Components of a Workplace Safety Plan

- Consider obtaining civil orders for protection and make sure that they remain current and are accessible at all times. A copy should be provided to the employee's supervisor, reception area, and security areas if there is a concern about the abusive partner coming to the work site.
- The employee should consider providing a picture of the perpetrator to reception areas and/or security.
- A company contact person should be identified for the employee to reach when needed.
- An emergency contact person should be identified should the employer be unable to contact the employee.
- Review the employee's parking arrangements for possible changes.
- Consider changing the employee's work schedule.
- Consider what steps need to be taken to provide for the safety of other employees and clients.
- Consider having the employee's telephone calls screened at work.

Selected Laws and Regulations

This appendix primarily focuses on laws and regulations as they apply to workplaces. Along with the selected list that follows, employers may want to learn more about general criminal laws (e.g., those covering assault, harassment and stalking) that can apply to workplace violence situations. If illegal acts occur in the workplace, an appropriate response involves law enforcement officials as well as administrative action.

Note that the laws and regulations detailed in this appendix are mandatory — as opposed to voluntary — for businesses subject to these legal requirements.

Late Night Retail Workers Crime Protection: WAC 296-832

The Late Night Retail Workers Crime Protection Standard provides specific violence-related direction to retail businesses that operate between 11:00 p.m. and 6:00 a.m. Restaurants, taverns, hotels and other lodging facilities are not covered by this rule.

The rule was created to improve the safety of workers in the late night retail industry. In general, the rule requires:

- Crime prevention training for workers.
- Safety measures, including drop safes and exterior lighting that remains on during all hours of operation.
- Signage announcing that workers cannot access the safe and that the cash register contains only the minimum amount of cash needed to conduct business.

To view the entire rule, visit **www.Lni.wa.gov/Safety** and look for Late Night Retail Worker Crime Prevention under "L" in the Index.

Safety in Health Care Settings: RCW 49.19

The safety in health care settings law requires employers in specific health care worksites to develop and implement a plan to reasonably prevent and protect employees from violence. The law requires that these plans include:

- A hazard assessment of the facilities.
- Training for employees on the workplace violence prevention plan.
- Follow-up on any workplace violence incidents that describes steps taken in response to the incident.
- A record of violent acts for at least 5 years from when the act is reported.

Workplace Violence Safety Plan in Public and Private Facilities for the Mentally Ill: RCW 72.23.400

This law requires employers in these settings to develop and implement a plan that would reasonably prevent and protect employees from violence. The plan must include:

- A hazard assessment of their facilities.
- Employee training on the plan.
- Follow up on any workplace violence incidents.
- A review of the plan at least annually.

Other L&I Regulations That May Apply to Workplace Violence Hazards

Several existing provisions of the Washington Administrative Code (WAC) may apply to the hazards of violence in the workplace, including (but not necessarily limited to) the following:

WAC 296-800-14025 requires employers "to establish, supervise, and enforce your accident prevention program in a manner which is effective in practice."

WAC 296-800-32005 requires employers to report fatalities and hospitalization of one or more employees to Labor & Industries within eight hours.

WAC 296-800-14005 requires employers to "develop a formal [written] accident-prevention program, tailored to the needs of the particular plant or operation and to the type of hazards involved." The program must include "a safety orientation program" that contains (among other things) information about reporting injuries and unsafe conditions, the use and care of personal protective equipment, and emergency procedures.

WAC 296-800-11005 requires employers "to furnish to each employee a place of employment free from recognized hazards that are causing or likely to cause serious injury or death" to employees. WAC 296-800-11010 requires employers "to adopt and use practices, means, methods, operations, and processes which are reasonably adequate to render such employment and place of employment safe" and to "do every other thing reasonably necessary to protect the life and safety of employees."

WAC 296-800-16005 requires employers "to assess the workplace to determine if hazards are present, or likely to be present, which necessitate the use of personal protective equipment (PPE)" and to select appropriate PPE and require its use.

WAC 296-800-310 requires "every building or structure, new or old, designed for human occupancy" to be "provided with exits sufficient to permit the prompt escape of occupants in case of fire or other emergency."

WAC 296-27-01101 requires employers to maintain records of occupational injuries and illnesses.

WAC 296-360-020 prohibits an employer from firing or otherwise retaliating against an employee for reporting unsafe work conditions, including concerns about potential workplace violence.

WAC 296-800-21005 requires "lighting which is adequately adjusted to provide a margin of safety for all work tasks" and specifies minimum indoor and outdoor lighting levels.

For details of existing regulations or policy that may apply to workplace violence hazards, contact the L&I service center nearest you.

Selected Laws Relevant to Workplace Violence

The following is a summary of selected federal and state laws that may relate to workplace violence issues in your workplace. The summary is not intended to be and should not be used as a substitute for specific legal advice. For legal advice consult your attorney or legal counsel.

Workers' Compensation

Whether an employer is self-insured or participates in the state fund, workers' compensation laws (RCW Title 51) are intended to compensate workers for injuries arising out of or in the course of employment. Generally, an employee is limited to the remedies offered under the workers' compensation laws and cannot bring a separate civil action unless evidence of an intentional injury is present.

Discrimination

Employers are prohibited from discriminating against employees on the basis of any protected characteristics. Both the Americans with Disabilities Act (ADA, 2 U.S.C. § 1202) and the Washington State Law Against Discrimination (RCW 49.60) offer job protection to "qualified individuals with a disability," including both physical and mental disabilities. If an alleged perpetrator of violence claims that his or her behavior is caused by a mental disability and requests accommodation of that disability, the employer must carefully weigh the options and outcomes of any decisions in dealing with that situation.

However, even if an employee's rude, insubordinate, or threatening behavior is caused by a qualifying disability such as clinical depression or a diagnosed mood disorder, that does not mean an employer has no options. The ADA only requires "reasonable" accommodation for individuals who are "otherwise qualified" for the position.

The ADA applies to employers with 15 or more employees. The Washington State Law Against Discrimination applies to employers with eight or more employees.

Tips for Reducing the Risk of Workplace Violence

When an incident of workplace violence occurs, an employer could face civil claims from three different parties: the victims, the violators, and even third parties, such as witnesses to the violence. These claims include but are not limited to negligent hiring, negligent retention, wrongful discharge, and failure to warn. Various measures an employer may take to limit potential liability are listed in the following pages.

Background Checks/References

Employers should check a job applicant's background as thoroughly as possible. Ask for complete prior employment history, education, and/or military service. Request that the applicant provide an explanation for any time gaps between jobs. Speak with previous employers regarding the applicant and any special concerns regarding the particular job in question.

Criminal Arrests and Convictions

The Washington State Human Rights Commission administers regulations covering fair and unfair pre-employment inquiries about arrests and convictions (WAC 162-12). Employers can ask applicants about criminal *convictions* that reasonably relate to the job duties of the position or request that information from the Washington State Patrol. Such inquiries can only address convictions or release from prison that occurred within the last 10 years. When employers inquire about arrests, they must ask whether charges are still pending, have been dismissed or led to a conviction of a crime involving behavior which would adversely affect job duties or the position. An arrest by itself is not a reliable indicator of criminal behavior.

Law enforcement agencies, state agencies, school districts, businesses and other organizations that have a direct responsibility for the supervision, care or treatment of children or vulnerable adults are exempt from these regulations. Thorough background checks are encouraged for positions that are particularly risky. In some cases, they are required for employers who provide care, supervision or treatment for children or vulnerable adults (RCW 43.20A.710, RCW 43.43.830-842, RCW 72.23.035).

As a matter of preventative employment practice, employers should include a disclaimer, such as "An arrest or conviction record will not necessarily bar you from employment with the company."

Credit Checks

A credit report can help to verify information on a job application. Include a statement in the job application form that indicates that credit checks will be performed and that the applicant agrees to allow such credit checks.

Washington has a Fair Credit Reporting Act. Under the Washington law, an employer may not take any adverse employment action based in whole or in part on information contained in a "consumer report" until it has advised the consumer against whom such adverse action is to be taken, supplied the name and address of the consumer reporting agency making the report, and given the consumer an opportunity to respond to any information in the report that is disputed.

Medical Examinations and Inquiries

The ADA prohibits employers from making medical inquiries into the health or condition of a current employee, except under the following conditions: (1) when the employee is having difficulty performing the job effectively; (2) when the employee becomes disabled, including on-the-job injuries; (3) when the employee has requested accommodation; (4) when required by other laws; or (5) in conjunction with voluntary health screening programs.

If an employee's behavior raises concerns for the employer because it is impacting job performance, the employer may require a medical examination or question the employee. However, the examinations or inquiries must be job-related and should focus on the employee's ability to perform the job. The employer should provide the medical professional with an updated job description so any analysis can focus on the essential job duties. The medical professional should address the nature of the condition, duties that the employee cannot perform, expected duration of the disability, necessary limitations on activity, and whether a potential threat to health and safety exists. Finally, the employee should sign a release of information to the employer.

Drug and Alcohol Testing

Although the ADA prohibits medical examinations that screen individuals for disabilities, a test to determine whether illegal drugs are currently being used is not considered a "medical examination" for the purpose of the ADA. (42 U.S.C. § 12114(d)(1)).

In contrast to tests for illegal drugs, blood alcohol tests, breath alcohol tests, and urine alcohol tests are considered medical examinations and are limited to those circumstances when medical exams are permitted when they are job-related and consistent with business necessity. (42 U.S.C. § 12112 (c) (4)(A)).

Workplace Searches

Public sector employers are governed by the right of privacy derived from the federal and state constitutional protections against unreasonable searches and seizures. The constitutional right hinges on whether the employer violates an employee's reasonable expectation of privacy.

Private sector employers generally may search on-property or employer-owned vehicles, desks, lockers, as well as packages, lunch boxes and the like brought to or taken from work. The employer should have a reasonable basis for any search and conduct the search in a reasonable manner. "Reasonable basis" does not include discriminating on the basis of race, sex, ethnic origin or other such characteristic. Employers may therefore wish to explain why any searches are necessary, establish search procedures that are minimally intrusive of employees' privacy, and ensure non-discriminatory criteria for searches are identified in advance and equitably applied. Inform employees that refusal to submit may lead to discipline or discharge for insubordination. However, avoid forcing employees to submit because detaining an employee involuntarily may lead to liability for false imprisonment.

Other Resources on Workplace Violence

Resources to develop a workplace violence prevention program, offer training for employees, or research the subject, are available from the state Department of Labor & Industries (L&I) and other sources.

L&I Safety & Health Video Library & Resource Center

L&I's Safety & Health Video Library & Resource Center has several videos on workplace violence available for loan.

Visit **www.Lni.wa.gov/Videos** to see a list of the available videos or call 800-574-9881.

Other Publications

Other publications are available on workplace violence. Many can be found by visiting **www.Lni.wa.gov/WorkplaceViolence**.

Internet Resources

Additional resources on workplace violence can be found at these websites:

- Washington State Hospital Association: **www.wsha.org**
- Occupational Safety and Health Administration: **www.osha.gov**
- Centers for Disease Control and Prevention, National Institute for Occupational Safety and Health: **www.cdc.gov/niosh/topics/violence**
- Oregon OSHA: **www.orosha.org**
- U.S. Bureau of Labor Statistics: **www.bls.gov**
- WorkSafe BC (British Columbia): **www.worksafebc.com**

Appendix G
Technical Assistance and Training

L&I provides free safety consultations to more than 2,000 Washington companies each year. Upon request, a safety and health consultant will visit any worksite and offer suggestions to improve safety, accident prevention programs and offer ways to save money on industrial insurance. The service is provided at no cost.

Safety consultants can also bring workshops to businesses upon request. Visit **www.Lni.wa.gov/SafetyConsultants** for more information or call 1-800-423-7233.

- For information in Spanish (Información sobre seguridad en español): **www.Lni.wa.gov/Seguridad**
- L&I website: **www.Lni.wa.gov**
- Safety and health information: **www.Lni.wa.gov/Safety**
- L&I forms and publications: **www.Lni.wa.gov/FormPub**

You can also call any of our regional offices for help:

L&I Regional Safety Consultants

Phone	Counties
425-290-1431	Island, San Juan, Skagit, Snohomish, Whatcom
206-515-2837	King
253-596-3917	Clallam, Jefferson, Kitsap, Pierce
360-902-5472	Clark, Cowlitz, Grays Harbor, Klickitat, Lewis, Mason, Pacific, Skamania, Thurston, Wahkiakum
509-886-6570	Adams (west county), Benton, Chelan, Columbia, Douglas, Franklin, Grant, Kittitas, Okanogan, Walla Walla, Yakima
509-324-2543	Adams (east county), Asotin, Ferry, Garfield, Lincoln, Pend Orielle, Spokane, Stevens, Whitman

PUBLICATION F417-140-000 [10-2015]

www.ingramcontent.com/pod-product-compliance
Lightning Source LLC
Chambersburg PA
CBHW081856280526
45789CB00007B/2721